I0150121

Femini Publishing

PUSSI POWER

Copyright © 2017 by Valerie Sherrod

Contents and/or cover may not be reproduced in whole or in part in any form without the expressed written consent of the author and/or publisher. This book is designed to inspire and activate feminine energy, humanitarian activists, and feminists.

The opinions expressed herein are solely the views of the author. The author represents and warrants that she either owns or has the legal right to publish all material in this book.

Unless otherwise indicated, all Scripture quotations are taken from the *Holy Bible, Good News Translation*®, © 1992 by American Bible Society. Used by permission. All rights reserved.

Scripture quotations marked (NIV) are taken from the *New International Version*®, © 1973, 1978, 1984, 2011 by Biblica, Inc.® Used by permission. All rights reserved worldwide.

ISBN-13: 978-0-9916122-5-3

Published by:
Femini Publishing and Enterprises
www.feminipublishing.com
valerie@feminipublishing.com

DEDICATION

I dedicate this book to women activists, feminists, philanthropists, and those who are on the front lines orchestrating change where necessary.

Who can find a virtuous woman,
for her price is far above rubies.
Prov. 31:10

ACKNOWLEDGEMENTS

TO HIS HIGHNESS

I feel blessed and honored to be alive and to be a part of your divine plan for my life. My Lord, your presence illuminates me and transports me to a place of spiritual intimacy.

By the grace of God, I am what I am.
I Corinthians 15:10

Contents

INTRODUCTION

My purpose for writing this book is to express the powerful feelings and insight that encompass a feminine woman. I want to ensure that each woman recognizes her self-worth, embraces her identity, and lives her truth as it is. As you realize your full potential as a woman, you will become unstoppable.

Being born a female is not a disadvantage! I wish I could go around and write this on every woman's palm as a reminder of her inner beauty and the power she possesses.

We live in a world defined as "a man's world." Based on this theory, women are considered second-class citizens, especially those living in male-dominated societies. With the advent of feminists everywhere, the value of women is rising to phenomenal proportions. Women are breaking glass ceilings that were once insurmountable. Should I say thanks to them? Somewhat. Feminists are raising their voices everywhere in hopes of equal rights for women. So our voices are not ignored, we are orchestrating change where necessary. We will continue to speak our truth until all women are free from antiquated systems that denigrate the global consciousness of humanity.

A woman is the most precious gift given to the world. She is a mirror image of all that is divine. Her femininity is a gift by The Divine One, as He who is divine created her to be powerful, yet soft. She is a force to be reckoned with, yet gentle and loving. Based on her position in heaven and on earth, she resembles wisdom and those who embrace her shall be blessed.

Do not abandon wisdom, and she will protect you,
Love her, and she will keep you safe.
Getting wisdom is the most important thing you can do.
Whatever else you get, get insight.
Love wisdom, and she will make you great.
Embrace her, and she will bring you honor.
She will be your crowning glory.
Prov. 4:6-9

CHAPTER 1

FEMININE ENERGY

To grasp the concept of the power of a feminine woman it is essential to recognize feminine energy. Feminine energy tends to be more receptive, yielding, and flowing. Mainly, it focuses on being rather than doing; or we can say it is doing without doing. A feminine woman concentrates on the process as well as the results achieved. Rather than acting in haste, she sees the big picture and plans wisely. Fate plays a major role in her affairs. When she surrenders to fate, she believes what is destined to happen, will happen.

Feminine energy is soft, but not docile. By exercising your feminine energy, you will:

➤ Be comfortable receiving and letting go of control
➤ Be playful
➤ Be vulnerable
➤ Fall in love with yourself
➤ Feel a quiet, yet powerful confidence
➤ Feel beautiful in your body

- ➢ Focus on what you desire and what makes you happy
- ➢ Speak your truth

From a business perspective, feminine leadership is more powerful because it welcomes emotions, builds consensus, and promotes understanding. The energy of female leadership supports and empowers others, especially when coupled with connecting and team building.

Some women rise to the position of leadership through skill, knowledge, and hard work. Others are anointed and appointed to be leaders. It is her divine nature. Whether she has a leadership title or not, her leadership skills are evident. She leads through divine guidance, wisdom, and love. Those who interact with her on a personal or business level reap the benefits by what she offers, whether it's her caring nature or words of wisdom.

Nobody wants a leader who creates a tense environment. An authentic leader detects potential in others and aids in the growth process. The ability to feel and appear serene and comfortable, even in a high-pressure environment, is the key personality trait of high-performing leaders. Another quality is her ability to cope with stressful situations and her innate ability to solve problems. Her power lies in being more relationship oriented. Characteristics such as nurturing, empathy, long-term perspective thinking, and networking are a few of her greatest assets.

Group intelligence correlates with the number of women on a team, according to MIT research. Retail stores with increased gender diversity witness a substantially higher revenue growth rate. The Fortune 500 companies with the highest percentages of female board directors produced 66% higher ROI on average.

Fifty percent of the world's population are women, and they affect about 85% of the purchasing decisions. Therefore, it is good business practice to include women in the design and innovation process. While thinking of an innovative ecosystem, envision communities with high levels of connectivity, collaborative sharing, and communication, which are, stereotypically, feminine traits.

Both genders rank feminine leadership traits as vital to solving the most pressing problems of today in government, business, education, and more. Now that's what you call power!

There's a resurgence of interest in feminine energy, particularly in dating books and sites. It is not a new concept by any means. However, it is not prominent in cultures who have embraced male energies of aggression, independence, confidence, and outward approach.

The women's movement was a badly needed one and helped women tremendously. Women were able to launch into areas that made them feel worthy, noticed, and successful. How did they do it? To bring balance, their role models taught them how to polish the masculine side of their nature.

Everyone embodies feminine and masculine energies. Historically, men tend to be more comfortable in traits commonly seen as masculine, *e.g.*, hunting and feeding the family. Nowadays, hunting business prospects and out thinking competitors are one of his common traits. Women were more comfortable in feminine energies, *e.g.*, receptiveness, nurturing, vulnerability, and relationship-based; the same energies that still impels women to take group trips to the ladies' room.

To work in a male-dominated world, outside a home, women had to evoke their masculine energy. Women who were the aggressive go-getters were labeled as "bitch" or "iron lady." It reached such extreme proportions that some women stopped valuing the feminine side of themselves and devalued activities such as housekeeping, nurturing and vulnerable behaviors. That's changing again. The nurturing and empathetic nature a woman has naturally is once again working in her favor. When she brings her talents and gifts to the forefront of mainstream society, the effects are apparent.

Ironically, social media and the accessibility of the internet has created a new business venue. A woman who desires the path of entrepreneurship can provide services, bring her talents to fruition, and sell or promote it via her own business with more ease than competing in a workplace that remains male-dominated.

Feminine energy manifests in different ways, *e.g.*, relationship building and empathy. These traits are helpful in client-focused businesses or situations where a mediator is needed. In addition, nurturing, organizing, and customer service skills are best used in administrative positions if that is her choice.

Small businesses, new marketplaces, and social media are all areas where a woman can bring her talents to the forefront and be successful. Women are also group driven, oriented and receptive by nature. As home-based businesses are beginning to flourish, and remote employment increases, these traits will serve her well. The possibilities are endless.

Feminine energy also travels through the global marketplace where women are recognized as global leaders and world changers.

In the end, both genders can exhibit feminine leadership qualities, but the propensity, both culturally as well as biologically, is for women to embody them more.

PHENOMENALLY FEMININE

My femininity

Is the light I need to track my path

Though the shadows of the world

Surround me,

I hold my head high,

And my womanhood higher,

Being soft in the hardest times,

It is my duty,

It is my pleasure.

Life,

Is nothing without the spark of a woman.

I am the miracle in the spirit of

Everything wholesome,

I am the whole of everything spirit,

My grace and my beauty are the tingles in the spine of

peace and love.

It may seem to you,

That it is hard for me to be this way,

Nevertheless, I cannot imagine living any less

phenomenally.

"She is clothed with strength and dignity and she laughs without fear of the future."
Proverbs 31:25

CHAPTER 2

FEMININE POWER

Different from masculine power, which develops things that are controlled and managed, feminine power creates things that are expressive, which our hearts deeply yearn. It could be love, intimacy, spiritual connection, self-expression, creativity, etc.

Express power and invoke change

WAYS TO HARNESS YOUR FEMININE POWER

In instances where feminine energy needs restoration and masculine energy balance, there are key ways to express power and invoke change.

Culturally, we relate masculine energy to planning and being results driven. It's about understanding where you want to go and get there as fast as possible.

At first glance, this approach sounds great; but it also enhances your vision by allowing you to strategize your next steps.

If you desire to create something beautiful, a vision board will aid in the process. Visualization helps by bringing your ideas into the material world. Articulate and focus on exactly what you would like to achieve when you see your target. By concentrating on the details and surrendering how it should manifest, you create the space to see something even greater than initially planned materialize.

What is the difference between embodying powerless feminine energy and overcompensating with masculine energy? Let's assume you're going on a date. If you feel powerless, you might say, "Wherever you decide to go is fine with me, you create the plans." Alternatively, you might just go with the flow without any input. Consequently, you would risk being disappointed and unhappy rather than having your needs met.

State your preferences, and let your feminine side take over.

The empowered feminine woman would engage by being communicative. Her communication style is soft but firm. She might say, "I like to eat healthy, clean food, so an eatery that caters to my eating habits would be beneficial. I also prefer outdoor seating with a scenic view." After you state your preferences, you both can agree on a place and allow

VALERIE SHERROD

your date to make the reservations. Dating works both ways, whether male or female.

Choose the power of connection and story-telling over rational debate.

Everyone knows how important a person's political views are. When debating policy and social issues, rationalization takes form. Both parties are adamant about their beliefs, and therefore each agrees to disagree. What if there was a way for both sides to reach an amicable agreement? What are the necessary steps without rationalization as the basis?

There is a technique called "canvassing." It changes people's perspective, especially concerning issues like gay marriage and abortion rights. This technique isn't executed by debating or appealing for freedom and equality. Instead, it is implemented by talking to people, sharing experiences, and probing why the issue is important to them. This is feminine power at its peak: it's about connection and emotion rather than analyzing and intellectualizing.

Both the beauty and advantage of inhabiting feminine power is the need to create change. By achieving your desires through plan execution, you unleash power, creativity, and connection as you walk in your divine feminine energy. These are the hallmarks of feminine power.

"You are altogether beautiful, my darling, beautiful in every way."

Song of Songs 4:7

VALERIE SHERROD

CHAPTER 3

WHERE DOES YOUR POWER LIE?

In today's world, there is a clamor for women to be given equal opportunities and recognition as their male counterparts. Feminism is the new world order. As the saying goes, "what a man can do, a woman can do equally," is being brought to life by women achieving great feats around the world.

Since women are within their rights to ask for equality, it must be understood that women were divinely orchestrated to rule and reign. She has been endowed with an inner strength which differentiates her from men and makes her stand apart. A woman is more than a person with female sex organs; she is a force to be reckoned with. She builds, nourishes, protects, defends, manages, encourages, and creates. She is the most unique creature to have walked the Earth.

Her power lies in her diversity, in her ability to function in one role and yet manages to function in multiple roles. A woman is dynamic, and like a chameleon—ever changing. She studies current market trends, and makes the necessary adjustments.

Her power lies in her strength. For centuries, women have served as protectors of their homes and countries. In modern-day society, women have been endowed with the superpower to manage their homes while working a nine-to-five job.

Her power lies in her conviction. When her convictions overrule theoretical thoughts, nothing will stand in her way.

The power to do whatever we want and be whomever we want, is a part of our self-confident mechanism. This is why women are thrusting forth in leadership arenas, we see the vision and run with it.

Her power lies in her fragility. Do you know there is strength in your fragility? Why not use it to your advantage. Powerful women do not fear their weaknesses because she understands that it is a part of her strength. By admitting to her weakness, she allows room for growth.

Her power lies in her determination. A woman who is determined will reach beyond the stars. Put obstacles in her way, and she'll either walk or jump over it to get to her destination.

Her power lies in believing in herself. Believing here connotes self-confidence and a woman with high self-esteem. As the saying goes 'there is nothing sexier than a woman who exudes self-confidence.'

When a woman embodies these traits, she becomes a superwoman capable of achieving anything. When she understands her power, she manifests. In manifesting, she conquers territories and rules like ancient and modern queens, instigating change where necessary. She knows there's no limit to what she can be because she is a woman and her power rests within her.

Honor her for all that
her hands have done,
and let her works bring her
praise at the city gate.

Proverbs 31:31

VALERIE SHERROD

Chapter 4

The Balance of Power

Men and women have the power to do what they think is right. Both live in a society where each has the freedom to do what they want and say what they think and feel, but bound by the laws and rules of that society.

Right from the onset, the masculine gender has always been seen as a symbol of power and authority in society. It goes without saying that the society we live in has always been a patriarchal one. This has in turn affected all areas of our life, relationships and careers.

In heterosexual relationships, it is widely believed and expected that women are to be submissive while the men are to be dominant. Lest "submitting" be misconstrued as slavery, inferiority or blind obedience, submitting actually means trust and acceptance. A woman trusts that what is asked of her is beneficial to the relationship and therefore accepts the request. The foundation for a woman's submission is actually not to a man, partner, mate, or husband, but to the one who created her. Submission, then, is a willful act of obedience to the Divine One.

In a relationship, competition shouldn't be an issue. Relationships should bring out the best in both partners. Partners are not limited by their strengths or weaknesses, because both can draw strength from each other. This is how balance of power is achieved.

Moreover, the concept of power balance is gradually creeping into relationships. Balance of power in a relationship means that there is a balance in the way each party in the relationship are getting their needs met. This means that no one feels cheated or unsatisfied as it is often the case in relationships where there is power imbalance.

The business world doesn't seem to be any different in regards to gender equality and balance of power between the sexes. For a while, important leadership traits such as assertiveness, dominance and linear thinking have been attributed to the male gender, while women are seen as emotional beings who cannot make brisk and ruthless decisions when placed in leadership positions.

However, it should be realized that several feminine traits, such as empathy, instinct and trust building skills are equally as important as the masculine traits. Good leaders would make use of their feminine and masculine sides to achieve the best results.

Over the past few years, we have witnessed more women rising to the power table in business. However, women still lag far behind as the population of women to men in business is still unequal.

Achieving balance shouldn't be depicted as supremacy of a particular gender against the other. Instead, it should be depicted as a learning tool to identify the uniqueness of each gender and unite to make society a better place.

I admire men who are on the front lines advocating for the rights of women and children. What a display of strength and support! The more virile a man is, the more receptive he is to feminine power. If he is very masculine, the more he appreciates feminine affection and care. A man's gruff voice finds a woman's soft voice soothing. When you see the union of both man and woman, there is sublimation – a state of being raised to a higher status. It does not mean, however, that a man or a woman alone is incomplete. Rather, the union of two different people is like merging two companies to form one partnership so it can reach its highest growth potential.

Overall, the balance of power between a man and woman goes beyond making myriad achievements. Instead, balance can exist when both parties make the most of what each has in service to others.

A Woman's Gift Makes
Room For Her
And Brings Her
Before Great Men
[paraphrased]
Proverbs 18:16

"God is within her, she will
not fall."

Psalm 46:5

VALERIE SHERROD

CHAPTER 5

SELF-CONFIDENCE

Where does confidence originate? How do you obtain it? Some believe it shows outwardly. I'm sure you have read, heard, or know people altering their appearance through surgical procedures to gain self-confidence. Plastic surgery has its benefits. I praise doctors who can use their skills to help others. However, physical attractiveness does not equate to self-confidence. Attractive people also face confidence issues. While looking good is great, the confidence you have in yourself is what attract others to you and will last when the outward beauty fades.

Women have made great strides throughout history. Until 1920, women were not allowed to vote. Today, some of us occupy top executive positions in Fortune 500 companies, while others have taken the entrepreneur route! While it is true that the fight for women to live their lives the way they want has proven successful, many still struggle with their own identity. This identity crisis manifests in the areas of low self-esteem and low confidence. A lack of confidence can stop us, and our lack of self-esteem hinders our ability to fulfill our dreams, to stand on our own and do great exploits. In theory, there are two options available. First, we can rise, take the initiative, and do something about it. Alternatively, we can sit on the sidelines and blame the patriarchy, our past, society, and whatever and whomever, for every obstacle on our path.

The first step to self-confidence is to accept yourself. The moment you accept your flaws (the things you can't change about yourself) the faster you will become more confident. Your flaw could be psychological, physical, or even financial. Maybe you don't have a perfect physique. Silence the inner critic who keeps telling you, your breast is too large or too small, your hips are not wide enough or too wide, your hair is not the right texture, or you are too short or too tall. The list goes on. You still are valuable. Right? Don't try to mask or hide your imperfection. Candidly, these things are a small part of who you are. If you accept your flaws, it won't be a big deal if others want to use it to crush you. Bullies and haters have no power over you.

Now that you have accepted yourself, the next step is to understand that only you have the authority to control what happens to you from now on.

You can't build confidence without fear. It is quite ironic when you think about it. You need the confidence to conquer fear. But you also need fear to build your confidence.

Do you find it difficult to interact with strangers? If so, attend an event that allows for networking. The event doesn't necessarily have to be a corporate setting. It could be a fundraiser, a charity event, a religious event, or a concert. Just dress appropriately for the occasion. Let people approach you for a conversation if you are afraid to start one. Listen intently and ask follow-up questions based on the discussion. Attend a new one every other week until you are comfortable in social settings. I can assure you that if you can overcome your initial fear of going to these places, you will overcome your shyness or fear of speaking in public.

The truth is those areas where confidence is lacking can be fixed with well-coordinated actions. Of course, you can't fix your family background or height, but you can fix your dietary habits. What's most important is doing it for the right reasons, not because you want to look like someone else. Do it because you want to be a better version of yourself.

When you excel at something, continue to do it. Whatever raises your self-esteem is encouraged, provided they are healthy practices.

Whatever you do, don't give up even if you fail a few times! Failure is a part of being successful. It teaches you how to revise your strategy to get the best results. Being the best version of yourself and raising your self-esteem is a journey. You can do it!

When you achieve your goals, celebrate yourself, even if your partner, spouse, or friends don't. Allow yourself some breathing space. Take yourself out and spoil yourself. Buy that dress you have always wanted. Go to that expensive restaurant and order a fancy meal. Visit places wealthy people visit just to have a feel of being wealthy. The motivation you will get can be transformational and may boost your esteem in two ways. It might make you want to work smarter to be wealthier, or it could change your perception of wealth, especially if you think it's unobtainable.

Celebrate the things that make you different. Are you a wife, a mother, a nurse, a boss, or a disciplinarian? Try changing your perception of what the traditional gender roles are. If you feel like working on your car engine, do it. If you want to fix your roof, fix it. If you want to ask someone out on a date, go ahead and ask. Get rid of whatever barrier society (or family and friends) has placed on your freedom. There is no greater confidence booster than identifying who you are as a feminine woman.

A person who lacks self-confidence often needs constant affirmation to feel good about themselves. Painful experiences of the past may have triggered these emotions. We have no idea what others endured in their lives or the obstacles they face daily. What I do know is "God heals and restores." Seeking therapy is also beneficial for your overall well-being. Whatever negative forces or energies that tried to destroy you, it didn't. You are still here! Repeat after me, "I will think good thoughts of myself. I will love me more than anyone else will. I have the power to make myself happy. I am responsible for my overall well-being."

We admire people who are self-confident because, not only are they fun people to be with, they also inspire confidence in others. They are brave individuals who get things done and tend to be optimistic about life. They have great respect for themselves and live a fulfilling life because they believe in themselves.

Wouldn't it be great to live such a life of fearlessness and faith in oneself? You can! Self-confidence is something that is achievable.

Self-confidence is a feeling of trust in one's abilities, qualities, and judgment; and, like all feelings, it comes from within. You have to trust yourself and believe you can achieve whatever you want. No one else will do it for you. If you don't believe in yourself, how do you expect others to believe in you?

Here are some tips for building self-confidence. Remember, self-confidence is an ongoing process. It is similar to a plant that needs nurturing.

TIPS FOR BUILDING SELF-CONFIDENCE

➢ Know who you are: Self-knowledge is an awareness of self that builds confidence. When you know your strengths, you can build on them. Know your weaknesses, too, and limit them. Logging this information in a journal will help you to remember them. So, the next time you doubt yourself, read your journal as a gentle reminder of your talents. You are an amazing cello player! You are an articulate speaker! But, how would you know unless you practice? By all means, do not listen to the voice of fear.

➢ Surround yourself with positivity: Positive thoughts inspire positive outcomes. The mind is a tricky thing. It tends to point to negatives more than it points to positives. Make it a goal to look on the positive side of everything. Also, surround yourself with positive people. The company we keep can make or break us. If your so-called friends tend to talk down to you, or always see the downside of things, maybe it's time to part with such friendships. If you want to nurture your self-confidence, you need people who are going to cheer you on rather than pull you down or drain your energy.

➢ Take Action: You think you can sing in front of a crowd, right? How lovely; now just try it! Taking baby steps is alright. You can start by gathering some friends together for karaoke night. It doesn't matter how many people show. What is important is you are taking action. As you progress, you will notice a boost in your confidence. Someday you will feel more comfortable singing in front of a crowd, just like you imagined.

➢ Be prepared: To be a confident, successful woman, you have to be willing to take on whatever tasks are before you. Self-confident people are hardworking individuals who invest time in themselves. Learn everything there is to know about your trade or business. Preparation is the key. When a student studies for an exam, he must read, conduct research, and learn all there is to know about the subject. When a student does not prepare, he will produce different results. Life has a way of preparing us for an exam. Sometimes we pass, and sometimes we fail. Have you ever noticed a cycle of events in your life? To obtain self-confidence, you will undergo a series of exams. Situations will arise that will deflate your self-esteem, and you will have two choices: 1) retreat and feel defeated, or, 2) raise your confidence level and walk in victory.

For me, abandonment by a parent at a young age was emotionally traumatizing. The inner scars seemed to become a permanent fixture in my heart that affected how I chose my companions. My self-confidence took a nosedive. I had to make some wise choices that would raise my confidence levels and enable me to take my power back. First, I surveyed my associations to detect who was really on my side. Who were the lifters and who were the energy vampires? The lifters can stay, all others EXIT STAGE LEFT. Next, I did an assessment of what I thought of myself, my life, and what I wanted from the two. Afterward, I committed to love myself first. I decided to do my best in life and keep growing, even if I stumbled. The patterns that contributed to self-sabotage were no longer welcome in my psyche. When my mind changed, my behavior changed. It is an ongoing process. When you decide to win in life, you become your champion. Believing in yourself is the ultimate mark of a self-confident woman.

In conclusion, you also gain power when you encourage and help other women. If you see other women in need, offer to help. By providing acts of service, we truly blossom and rise to our most powerful self.

So, there you have it, the recipe to getting the power to be YOU. Let's start now.

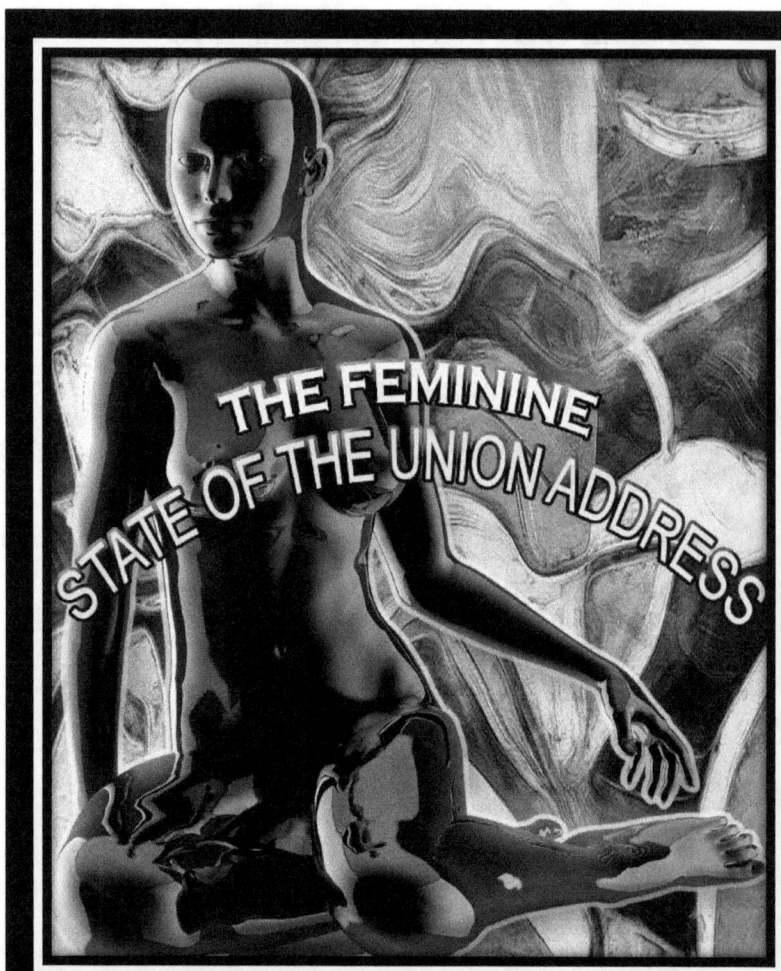

THE FEMININE
STATE OF THE UNION ADDRESS

THE FEMININE STATE OF THE UNION ADDRESS

UNITED WE STAND - GLOBALLY WE WIN

WE WILL NOT BOW TO:

- global economic injustices
- global systems/institutions of gender inequality
- global institutions of enslavement
- global hegemony
- high political seats of exclusion
- subversive desensitization

We bow only to the Divine. The Divine One has come to restore order. According to the original blueprint for women, we are equal with men but opposite in gender. We were created to rule and reign together.

NAMASTE

For the divine hath created a new thing in the earth: a woman shall encompass a man (surround, shield, love and protect)
Jer. 31:22

Feminist Revolution

How can I start a feminist revolution?
When our little girls across the world
Are getting executed
Put up for sale – Stamped and redistributed

Does the constitution recognize their rights?
Oppressors traffic teens through their institutions
Don't want women's rights but support executions
While forces denigrate cultures with vast pollution
All alone left shackled in destitution
Was this the way to go about evolution?
Wash away the sins from the past with ablutions

I'm unapologetically a woman
Trying to search for solutions
Sometimes feel excluded while voicelessly muted
Posing as a lady in this socially constructed illusion
Fighting through the wars of the mind – moral
delusions
Why do the wicked thrive while the good remain
persecuted?

I want to save our girls what's your contribution
PTSD of the sex trade generating mind contusions
Many lies crafting up conspiracy reigns unproven

We must give power back to the women
Or our birthers will be in ruin
A man's world while we stay Venusian
To live in harmony, we must have peace of mind
Because the cost of peace
Gives birth to our humanity.

Chapter 6

Do you have what it takes?

Women have endured injustices on many levels. We have wept in our silence, but we endured. We have been sidelined in economic matters, but we persevered. We have been relegated to the kitchen in some regions of the world, but we found a way to turn lemons into lemonade. Many would like for us to keep quiet and stay in our place. Our place? We have no limits!

We have the right to speak
We have the right to be heard
We have the right to be feminine
We have the right to nurture and be nurtured
We have the right to defend ourselves from all forms of abuse
We have the right to exercise our full power whenever we deem necessary!

Feminine Essence

Your feminine essence is the core of who you are and mainly what will direct you when you need guidance.

In the direst circumstances, women have emerged with the strength to prevail. Believed by some to be the weaker vessels, we have learned to transform our weaknesses into strength. Our inner strength is delicate yet very powerful and unique. It is what differentiates women from men. Some women have misplaced their femininity or have forsaken it entirely in exchange for a masculine approach. Does a woman need to prove that she can be like a man? You, my dear lady, were not created to be like a man. You were created to be loving, soft, gentle, kind and fierce. Never miss opportunities to showcase these qualities in a quest to prove that you can function better in a place where you are not meant to function.

Your femininity is your greatest asset as a woman. Often, it is seen as sexiness, however it has a greater aspect. It is the glory that radiates from you when you are around others. It is similar to looking at the sun after the rain. When people come into your presence, they will notice something different about you.

Feminine energy emanates from you, which commands attention wherever you go. The feminine essence of a woman is her aura, which gives her the power to be herself. Every woman possesses feminine power, but it must be released. How is it released? It is released through your energy. When you exude confidence, self-assurance, soundness of mind and positive traits, you can bring yourself to a place of greatness. You decide how, when, where, why and to whom you release your power. After all, it is your power! Contrarily, if you are in a co-dependent state and have given others too much power over you, it is time to TAKE IT BACK! In doing so, allow wisdom to be your guide. Return to you, refresh yourself, love again, live again, and transform yourself from the inside out. You are worth it!

I wish all women embrace their feminine essence. The earlier you start the better. You are a gift to humanity.

Economic Injustice

Some erroneously assume that women are advocating for equal rights to compete with men.

This assumption is egregious. Women are not competing with men. What we are fighting against are systems and economic injustices that have penetrated into the global consciousness of our society, making women feel undervalued. This is an external fight, but there is also an internal fight. The inner struggle to create a path that leads to our ultimate economic success is compromised. When we fail to explore our full potential, that which could catapult us into the limelight of a more rewarding economic standing (both within society and ourselves), we hinder our growth process.

Women who are still dependent upon an economic system that has so many limitations, will always be subject to economic injustice. Some of us are the cause of our misfortune because we have failed in creating economic justice for ourselves.

Economic justice occurs when you depend upon the economic system that you have created for yourself.

> *"Do the best you can until you know better. Then when you know better, do better."* ~Maya Angelou

Masculine Energy

Masculine energy is vital for every woman. It is different from physical energy; rather, it centers on how you creatively energize yourself to achieve your goals. What drives you? Are you enthusiastic about reaching your goals? Feminine energy is essential. It allows you to multitask. However, feminine energy in the absence of masculine energy is incomplete. A lack of masculine energy makes the feminine energy appear weak, unappreciated, unfocused, unsupported, unstable, scattered, and purposeless. As a result, the foundation for success is incorporated by balancing both energies.

Masculine energy has a natural ability to take action. It pushes the woman into achieving her goals. It is analytical, concrete, assertive, controlling, active, and logical which compensates for any imbalance in feminine energy. Feminine energy alone is not sufficient for success in today's world. A woman must be able to balance both energies in her daily life.

Inequality

Inequality is witnessed throughout the world. Despite the giant strides that women have made in society, including the workplace, there is still a worrying persistence of inequality. Bridging the gap is a demanding but necessary responsibility. First, there is a necessity for men to be incorporated into the theoretical system. There have to be general discourses on how institutions, workplaces especially, benefit everyone, not excluding any gender.

Today, women have achieved high educational success. However, challenges arise as women struggle to balance work, family, and the added responsibility of caregiving. In these circumstances, women will often devote more time to household activities and less time into the workplace. In this case, gender equality won't be possible, especially when women are required to spend more hours at the workplace but are unable to. One way to bridge the gap is to equally divide the household responsibilities, or hire help if necessary.

Other ways to close the gap include standing up for your rights, raising awareness, sponsoring a child in need, involving yourself in politics, or being an activist. Each of these methods will help further the fight for equality for women, especially in areas where there is little education or awareness. Using your position or status to help bring about awareness in certain regions (for example, in developing nations in the Middle East and Africa) will contribute to reducing inequality among women globally.

Nurturing Yourself

Nurturing yourself should be at the top of your bucket list. Often, we neglect ourselves at the expense of caring for others and putting others' needs before ours. However, knowing how to nurture ourselves is of utmost importance to our overall wellbeing.

First, we must learn to put aside our worries. Focusing on reading an interesting book can help relieve stress. In addition, adventuring outside of our routine, *e.g.*, swimming, cycling, or exercising, can bring a sense of calm. No matter how we feel, thankfulness should be a part of our daily devotion. Express gratitude for who you are and what you have. When did you last eat that delicious recipe you always enjoyed as a child? Why not taste it again? Smile even if you are not in the mood. Find ways to make yourself happy.

Nurturing ourselves helps to restore balance in our lives. Through inner reflection, we can get rid of distractions and take inventory of our lives. By doing so, we will discover what makes us happy, sad, or indifferent. Journaling is another avenue to reveal our likes, dislikes, and the things we are ambivalent about. Can you think of ways to nurture yourself? Always endeavor to make time for yourself, because you deserve it.

Also, you can use these ideas to nurture others around you.

Invest in Yourself

Investing in yourself is an important aspect of being a woman. Learning the art of meditation is a great start. By feeding your inner person, you set the stage for investing, and allow yourself to focus on your needs and desires. What will it take for you to be happy and healthy? When we stop, think, and decide what we want to do with our lives, and what is best for us, we set out on a course of personal fulfillment. You should come first before anything else, including a family, job, or other responsibilities.

While investing in ourselves, we can create new ideas by focusing on our interests. These could be computer programming, painting, or writing. Only concentrate on the things that interest you.

Networking is another avenue. You have to learn to meet people even if you are shy. Networking has the propensity to help you acquire new ideas and get help when you need it most. Also, it would expose you to the myriad of opportunities around you. Finding ways to connect is easier than you think.

Another way to invest in yourself is by educating yourself. This doesn't necessarily mean going back to school, although you could return to school if you choose to. You can educate yourself simply by working with someone (*e.g.*, mentor), doing what you are interested in, or reading a book. You could also use the internet to search for topics that interest you or engage in educative conversations with people.

Are you investing in yourself financially? How much money do you save? Before spending money on anything else, pay yourself first. By deducting a percentage of your resources, you will see a noticeable difference in a few months or a year. The extra savings can be used to travel, buy a new car, and invest in stocks or education. Seek professional assistance if this is not one of your strong areas.

Finally, learn to spend time where it matters. Using your time wisely is another great way to invest in yourself. If possible, delegate some of your projects while spending time on other important things, *e.g.*, exercising regularly. Exercising will keep you mentally and physically fit and ensures that you stay focused on one activity. Examples of exercises that you can do include walking, jogging, running, swimming, weightlifting, CrossFit, jumping rope, using cardio machines, cycling, etc. Also, listening to music is an excellent way to spend time alone. It is a de-stressor which allows you to multitask. Both methods are great ways to invest in yourself.

Namaste
I bow to the Divine within you.

Emotional Freedom
Emotional freedom is essential for every woman, which involves healing hurts and disappointments of the past. This could be the death of a loved one, a job loss, or a lost relationship. Let go of any offenses that you have harbored against yourself or others. Grieving over such things for too long or bearing grudges will only weigh you down. You must learn to forgive because this is what will give you inner peace after someone hurts you. It will also help to stabilize your emotions and keep your mind at ease. In this way, you will be able to focus on whatever is of utmost importance to you, whether it's work, school, or hobbies. You will also be able to discharge your duties more efficiently to achieve optimum results. Moving on and learning to do great things is a sure way to invest in yourself.

In conclusion, this chapter has explained in detail some characteristics and virtues that make women complete. A grounded woman does not see herself as a victim of economic injustice. She creates economic justice for herself by utilizing her talents and gifts to the maximum. She does not depend on financial systems that exclude her but creates one for herself. A grounded woman possesses feminine and masculine energy and is focused, stable, energetic, nurturing, purposeful, and balanced. She does not allow distractions to overtake her. A grounded woman does not fear inequality but strives to achieve her goals. She nurtures herself regularly to make use of opportunities that come her way and utilizes them to her advantage. Investing in herself is not an option but a necessity. She reads to educate herself, networks with people, saves and invests money, spend time where necessary, and exercises regularly. She also gives herself emotional freedom by letting go of her past and focusing on important things that will lead to her ultimate satisfaction in life.

> *"I have the nerve to walk my own way, however hard, in my search for reality, rather than climb upon the rattling wagon of wishful illusions."*
> *~ Zora Neale Hurston*

She is a breath of God's power—a pure and radiant stream of glory from the Almighty. Nothing that is defiled can ever steal its way into Wisdom. She is a reflection of eternal light, a perfect mirror of God's activity and goodness. Even though Wisdom acts alone, she can do anything.

Wisdom 7:25-27

CHAPTER 7

BORN TO BE A GODDESS

Women who know their worth do not settle for anything less than their value. They walk with a divine purpose in mind. When a woman doesn't know her worth, she will settle for less than her value. Prayerfully, I hope that your mind will transcend into an awareness of who you truly are.

A goddess walks with purpose. As she moves forward, people swing into action. She knows the power she possesses and uses it wisely. Her actions portray her virtue. She carries herself with poise and doesn't involve herself in situations that would compromise her integrity.

You are a goddess. Yes, you! You were custom made from a place of divine royalty. Goddesses deserve worship. You should be treated with care and love. Surround yourself with those who possess these qualities. We must always remind ourselves of who we are and the contributions and sacrifices we have made to better ourselves, our families and our communities. Women are an integral part of communities, both locally and globally. Nothing in this world can function without the help of a woman. Your worth is invaluable. Recognize the goddess within you and use it to your advantage.

I pray for all women to exercise her feminine strength by using her power to eradicate antiquated systems that no longer serve her or humanity.

Goddess, you were born to rule and reign your world. According to history, women were to rule and have dominion. Through deception, that power was taken away but not destroyed. She would eventually reclaim her power to retain her goddess status, but with a hefty price to pay. You have everything you need to rule your domain. Your domain is an area in your life you have decided to conquer. Do not stop until you have achieved just that.

VALERIE SHERROD

Chapter 8

Abuse

Abuse: To use wrongly or improperly; misuse

Women are not put on this Earth to be enslaved or to tolerate abuse in any form. If you are in an abusive situation, please seek help immediately. In a situation where boundaries are crossed, they are put in place for protection. When protective barriers are dismantled, unlawful acts are demonstrated.

Exploitation

Abuse can take various forms, including sexual exploitation. Sexual exploitation exists because it occurs without both parties' consent.

Between marital couples, sexual exploitation occurs when one partner refuses to have intimate relations with the other. Being married does not give spouses the right to abuse each other. Therefore, if the sexual act does not take place with mutual consent, it is considered abuse.

Abusers use constraints, threats, mental and emotional manipulation, and various other methods to stir fear and submission in their victims. Their only motive is gratification and other sick interests.

Unfortunately, there are numerous cases in which children become the victims of sexual exploitation, especially when a family member who should care for and protect them violates them. This makes the child feel insecure and threatened in the place where he or she should feel completely safe. Sexual exploitation is also used to create footage that fuels the world of pornography where the exploiter advantages financially by selling such footage.

Regardless, sexual exploitation will always leave deep scars on its victim. The impact on children and teenagers can seriously affect his/her development. The violation severely damages a child's mental and physical health, their training and education, family relationships, social relationships, their connections with friends, and the way they view others. Futuristically, it can damage their relationship with their children. So, everything related to their life is altered causing serious problems that trigger psychological repercussions (*e.g.*, depression, anxiety, low self-esteem, nightmares, eating disorders, self-harming behaviors, and the feeling of being an outcast).

Therefore, it is essential, especially for children, to get professional help immediately (spiritual and practical). Without proper support, children will become dysfunctional members of the community, unable to integrate, follow a destructive lifestyle, or become perpetrators themselves. Some consider committing suicide, consumed by the thoughts of being worthless and unaccepted. Also, the abused can become pregnant, contract sexually transmitted diseases, or suffer physically from long-term injuries. In the case of teenagers, violence can push them towards drug addiction, such as excessive alcohol consumption and drugs, which will further deteriorate their health and life quality.

But there is light at the end of the tunnel. Resources such as counseling, therapy, and faith-based organizations are great ways to begin the healing process. You win in the end!

Human Trafficking

Human trafficking is nothing but slavery. Some victims are deceptively brought from developing countries with shallow standards of living to rich countries that promise better living and better jobs. Upon reaching their destination, they are subjected to various forms of labor. The victims are mostly women and children. It is rather unfortunate that the originator of some trafficking cases is an acquaintance of the victims and their family.

Children are subjected to forced labor while women are subjected to prostitution. The United States is the destination country for over 50 percent of human trafficking cases. According to a recent statistic, more than 18,000 people are trafficked into the United States from more than 50 different countries each year. More than 130 countries encounter human trafficking as origin country, transit country or destination country. This is not the only disturbing figure about trafficking. More than 300,000 children are trafficked into and within the United States every year.

These traffickers want to make a fortune on its victims by charging much less for sex than what average prostitutes charge. Therefore, they are subjected to laborious duties. Women are forced to have intercourse with as many men as possible. In fact, some women satisfy up to 30 people per day. This is where the real exploitation lies. The victims don't get paid for their services. Rather, their "pimp" receives the money.

When any of the victims can no longer work either because of ill health or due to other reasons, they are subjected to physical and psychological torture. Some contract rare diseases and thereby sent home. This trauma has also led to the death of many human trafficking victims. These traffickers operate as a syndicate and in secrecy. This operation is shrouded in so much secrecy that it could be happening next door to you. We all have to be vigilant.

Most importantly, let's do what we can to discourage that act of subjecting kids to manual labor. Whenever you see a child subjected to any forced labor, please report it. It is our responsibility to fight human trafficking.

The case of human trafficking is an enormous crisis that has evolved into a human rights issue. It is usually slavery without an end. It will continue to thrive as long as there is a market for supply and demand. All of us have a role to play. What will you do?

DIVINELY FEMININE

To be woman
Is
To be love.
The divinity in femininity
Is the child of nature and the heart.
We are everything beautiful
Because beauty cannot be born without a
womb.
Nothing can.
We exist because of divinity
The all-powerful one
Breath of life
Wind blows into my soul
I came out
Kicking, screaming, and befuddled,
Crawling towards nurturance,
Pining for a drop of the only love powerful
enough to bring forth life.
We are the ink in the pen,
Everything we touch is filled full of creation
and love,
The kind to send the spirit into ecstasy,

The kind to create universes.

VALERIE SHERROD

Chapter 9

A Harlot to the Rescue

In the desert, water symbolizes life and sand symbolizes death. Where the two touch, beautiful oasis' spring out of the barren soil, producing a burst of color, wonder, and food. The ancient town of Jericho is a perfect example of how much beauty there is to be found, even in the most desolate of places, if only there is water. Called the "City of the Palms," Jericho is a lush settlement situated next to the river Jordan, in the land of Canaan. The chosen ones will reach this Promised Land after wandering in the desert for 40 years. In Jericho is where Rahab lived, her house is an inn embedded into a part of the city's outer wall.

[A Story within a Story]
"Rahab, bring me two more drinks," yelled a haggard man with a raspy voice. "That is, two more for me and two for my friend!" He burst into laughter and slapped the man next to him on the back. His friend slouched on the table, his head buried in his arms, in the kind of dead slumber that nothing could wake him. Rahab looked at her

nephew, who already filled four cups with ale and gave him a quick nod. Her nephew clinched the cups, pulled them to his chest and scurried to the table. "He's learning quickly," Rahab thought and smiled faintly.

Despite running a decent business, Rahab couldn't shake off the vicious rumors of being a harlot. That kind of gossip tends to follow a person, no matter where they go and what they do. In the end, one only stops fighting them and starts living life as it is. "We wear our life as a coat, with the past days dragging behind us as a coattail and they bother us at every turn. It's rare that we get a chance to drop our old coat and take on a new one," Rahab thought just as two strangers walked into the Inn.

One was an older man with a worn, blue cloak and the other a young man in a brand new, fiery red cloak. The cheery mood quickly died down as everyone in the Inn looked at the door and tensed up. Rahab later wondered if the two spies intended their arrival to be known.

Rahab approached them, her hips swaying seductively, "My name is Rahab, and I welcome the weary travelers. Make yourself comfortable and feel free to order a drink or meal. If you can afford it, of course."

The two men stood in silence for a moment, but then the older one spoke, "My name is Caleb and this is Gaddi. Our people have come to claim our Promised Land, the land of milk and honey. So, the LORD has promised, and so the LORD shall deliver." Gaddi spoke through his teeth, "We're sick and tired of the desert. Our people deserve a proper home!" Caleb placed a hand on his shoulder and said, "It's alright, calm down. I think we'll have two drinks and a meal, as long as it's hot."

Rahab examined their faces with her piercing brown eyes. Caleb's face was creased and folded as if through the desert wind mistook it for a dune and shifted it back and forth with gleeful abandon. But, it exuded serenity, and his hazel eyes calmly observed Gaddi's reaction at every turn. On the other hand, the young man had a smooth face framed by a set of angry eyebrows and tightly pressed lips. He clenched his fists every so often, readying himself to fight against the entire world all by himself.

The two chose a table and sat down. Rahab felt the sudden urge to sit down with them. She was so transfixed that a haggard man slipping out the backdoor went by her completely unnoticed. She signaled her nephew to get them two ales and a hot meal, and he nodded in compliance.

Rahab was well versed in the inn-keeping business and knew that people often have the urge to overcome the silence by sharing what's on their minds, so she sat there patiently. It didn't take long for Caleb to start talking about their ordeals.

"We've been through thick and thin in the past 40 years that we've escaped Egypt across the Red Sea. The LORD has led us through water and fire and promised a land of our own, where we can finally settle. Canaan is this land of milk and honey. We intend to take it."

Gaddi hissed, "We'll destroy everyone who stands in our way, for we are the LORD's chosen people. We carry the Ark of the Covenant that can perform miracles."

Caleb motioned with his hand to quiet him down, but Gaddi kept talking, "There were tests, of course. Our faith was tested all along the way. I even had to do some unspeakable things with my own two hands. The LORD works in mysterious ways." With that, he went quiet and gazed into his own two hands, which lay crossed on the worn timber of the inn table.

Rahab had a sudden realization that this is what faith can accomplish. The chosen ones have endured decades of tribulations in the desert, wandering across kingdoms in search for their Promised Land, and they ended up in Canaan. Caleb and Gaddi were complete opposites, but also two sides of the same coin, with both anger and devotion being valid attitudes.

She had never experienced anything like it. Sure, everyone worshipped whichever idol or spirit they wanted in Jericho, but there was no such fervor and devotion in the eyes, faces, and words of these two men. It felt that faith like this one could move mountains and indeed perform miracles.

A sudden sound of clopping outside the inn interrupted Rahab's train of thought. She snapped out of her daydreaming and realized the city guard had arrived. Someone tipped them off, and they must be in search of the chosen ones.

Rahab immediately set into action, "Quickly, hide on the roof!" She motioned to her nephew, and he raised the ladder to the hatch leading to the attic. Caleb and Gaddi jumped to their feet and ran up the ladder, pulled it up behind them, and closed the hatch. Right in time, as the front door opened and two heavily armed guards entered the inn. "Where are the spies?" snarled one guard as he grabbed Rahab by the throat.

Words gurgled out of her mouth, "They were here, but I had no idea they were spies, let alone the chosen ones. They had a meal, some ale, and went out in a hurry," she said, pointing towards the table where they were sitting just a minute ago. The other guard approached the table and touched the bowl. "It's still warm; they must have just left."

Rahab felt the grip on her throat ease up and took a deep breath. The guard got in her face and said, "Where did they go?" Rahab felt her sarcastic attitude return and replied with a smug smirk, "If they had any brains in them, probably outside the city. As you know, the city gates are closed shut at dusk." The guard frowned, turned towards the one next to the table, motioned with his head towards the door, to which he ran out to catch the spies. Then he again turned to Rahab, "If we find out you've hidden the spies, you'll pay. That's a promise by the king, harlot."

Rahab said, "They seemed like any other traveler to me, and their money was good, so I took them in. What was I supposed to do? Besides, the more time you waste here with me, the less likely you are to catch them. And the king probably won't like that." The guard squinted, examined Rahab's face for a few moments, then squeezed through his teeth, "This isn't over," and rushed out the door. Suddenly, rapid clopping was heard on the pavement, and silence again came over the inn. Rahab hooted a huge sigh of relief and collapsed into the nearest chair. She felt all the stress and anxiety of those few moments in an instant, and her body started shaking uncontrollably. But this wasn't the first time she had an unpleasant experience with the city guard, so she quickly recovered, approached the ceiling hatch, and carefully called out, "It's alright, they're gone. You can lower the ladder now."

Do you have a past that haunts you? A shadow that just won't go away. Guess what? We all have something in our past that we would not like to disclose. But, that's why it's called the past. It is behind you. Yes, some people will not let you forget it. That's their problem, not yours. You have been positioned to live again; you get a second chance, a third chance, and so forth. As long as we live, each day teaches us principles to live by and personal development exercises that test our faith. I am not all I want to be, but I'm sure not what I use to be. One day at a time. But you must believe.

THE BEAUTY OF A WOMAN

No matter the rules of society
Every woman is beautiful inside and out
No need to freak out and have anxiety
Because every woman is amazing without a doubt
With women there is always variety
So feel free to stand out

Don't listen to what people say
You should always be yourself
When someone's words lead you astray
Put yourself on the top shelf

To live as a woman in today's society is hard
Wear this not that
Be this not that
Be unique but not that unique
Be yourself but don't act like that
It's hard to break free of the rules that we face
But no matter what anyone tells us
We are all beautiful inside and out
You don't have to look like a model
To achieve your greatest dreams
All you need is a good head on your shoulders
And a heart full of confidence
You don't need to follow what society says
Because as a woman you can do anything
The power of a woman
Doesn't come from her appearance
It doesn't come from her body-hugging dress
Or her five-inch heels
Or the amount of makeup on her face

VALERIE SHERROD

The power of a woman
Comes from the way she carries herself
It comes from her personality
And how she looks at the world
And how she handles problems
The power of a woman comes from within

As a woman
You have power
You have the power to do anything you want
You can be a mother or you don't have to
You can wear makeup or not if you don't want to
You can wear pants
If you're not into skirts and dresses

As a woman
You have the power to be anything you want
You dress the way you like to dress
You act the way you want to act
You have the power to control your own life
And create your own destiny
Don't let the words of others get you down
Your life is your life not anyone else's
As a woman
You can dress to your liking
You can dress your body any way you want
As long as you feel comfortable

As a woman
You can be
KIND
GENEROUS

CONFIDENT
DETERMINED
Believe it or not
Beauty exists inside and outside

There's a myth that says
That women can only be beautiful
On the inside or the outside not both
But as a woman you can be both
You can change your physical appearance
To fit your own standards of beauty
You can mold your personality
To fit your standards of beauty
You can still look beautiful
While having a beautiful personality
And who says that
Women can only be beautiful
In one place but not both

VALERIE SHERROD

CHAPTER 10

A QUEEN ON A MISSION

[A Story within a Story]

No matter where the chosen ones lived, they kept to themselves and always considered the LORD the ultimate authority. Their loyalty attracted the anger of many rulers, who feared and loathed their religious fervor. On one occasion, a man refused to prostrate himself in front of Haman, a Persian noble. Seething with rage, Haman asked Xerxes, the Persian king, to pay for the privilege of wiping out the entire tribe from Persia, which he granted. But Queen Hadassah would learn of this plot and intervene to save her people from certain destruction.

Queen Hadassah was painting next to an open window as one of her maids sat motionless, holding a bowl of fresh fruit. The birds chirped in the palace garden, and the light breeze carried with it a gentle fragrance of roses. But, a haggard figure in the distance attracted her attention.

"Hathak, who is that man sobbing in front of the palace gate? I've been seeing him for several days now," said Hadassah to her trusty eunuch. "It's Mordecai, the chosen one," he said. "Haman ordered him to show respect, and he refused. Hence, Haman pleaded with King Xerxes to order the destruction of all immigrants in his kingdom in 11 months' time. The royal edict has already been sent out."

Upon hearing this, Hadassah's heart froze and her hairbrush dropped out of her hand. She said, "My people, doomed to destruction, with no one to intervene on their behalf!" Hathak's eyes were wide open, "You are one of them-" but then he quickly composed himself and added, "my queen?" Hadassah said, "It's true. I haven't declared myself to the king because I feared what he would think of me. Hathak, have I ever done you wrong? Our actions speak louder than words and they testify who we are. Tell me, have I treated you kindly?"

Hathak bowed his head and said, "You have, my queen. Your words and actions towards your other servants and me are with utmost grace. I trust your judgment and will do as you command." Hadassah said, "Lend me your ear. How can I petition the king to save my people?"

Hathak shook his head, "None may approach the king without being summoned. The penalty for doing otherwise is death. The king does as he pleases." Hadassah smiled, "If I can't petition the king, perhaps he can be made to request me first. Quickly, bring me my finest robes!"

Hadassah walked in the king's view until he got curious and pointed at her with the golden scepter, which was a sign she could approach him. Xerxes said, "Hadassah, my beautiful queen, why are you so restless? What does your heart desire? Say your wish, and I shall grant it to you."

Hadassah sighed, "My king, I don't want to bother you with such trifles." Xerxes' curiosity was piqued, "Tell me, my beloved Hadassah." She sighed again and said, "My king, I shall arrange for a banquet tonight and explain everything. I humbly request that Haman be present as well." Xerxes clapped his hands, "So be it!"

During the banquet, Hadassah revealed Haman as a threat to her and her people, invoking the rage of Xerxes, who ordered him executed and gave his estate to Mordecai. Unable to rescind his royal edict, Xerxes issued another one, allowing all immigrants to defend themselves from any attacks on the day they were to be destroyed and the day after. From that day on, the memory of Queen Hadassah, and how she saved her people has won her recognition by many.

What is your mission queen? What were you placed on this Earth to accomplish? Like Hadassah, your moment to reveal who you are will come at a time when you least expect it. There's more to you than meets the eye. You were chosen by a higher source for a particular purpose. Hadassah refused to sit back and watch those she was destined to reach destroyed. Her passion was stronger than her fears. The beauty of this story is she was surrounded by mentors to help her fulfill her mission. Each one of us can make a valuable contribution, but the first contribution must be to yourself. You got this!

CHAPTER 11

ORDINARY JUST WON'T DO

Joan of Arc was just a simple farm girl born in France in the 15th century when the country was torn apart by the English conquest (which had lasted for nearly a century at that point). The usurpers had all but secured the French throne when this deeply pious girl appeared, claiming she was in contact with the LORD, who commanded her to lead the French to victory and unification, just as an ancient prophecy foretold. But her parents had something else in mind.

[A Story within a Story]

"Dad, I'm not marrying anyone!" said Joan defiantly. Her father could see her nostrils flaring up, which usually meant she wasn't going to budge this time. He had no idea what thoughts arose in her mind.

"Honey, the baker boy will treat you well. You're already 16, and besides, your mother and I would like grandchildren as soon as possible," he said, glancing at his wife, who was sewing next to the window. She stopped her work and looked at Joan, who could see a glisten in her eyes, without saying a word.

For a moment, Joan imagined herself leading an ordinary life, without wars, prophecies, or conquests. She suddenly thought about having a family, smiling naughty children that would always get away without punishment, and a handsome husband who would come home from work every day to lift her by the waist and shower her face and neck with kisses.

That fantasy lasted for a mere moment, as the visions returned, stronger and clearer than ever before. Now there was no doubt in Joan's mind that only a few chosen ones get to have the unique honor of having been born with a purpose. Hers was to lead France to liberation and victory.

"I am going to see the deposed French king, I will convince him that I can lead his army to victory, and I will do it," said Joan calmly.

Her father's face was drooping with sadness, "War is a terrible thing. Men die every day in war if they're lucky."

"I am not afraid," said Joan, "I was born to do this."

Father spread his arms and said, "Alright then, I'll arrange for you to see the town's council and convince them as you've convinced me." So, he did.

VALERIE SHERROD

Joan already had the mindset of a warrior, and now she changed her appearance to match it by cutting her hair and wearing men's clothes. She convinced the dejected French king to give her command over what remained of the French army, and she lead them to a monumental victory that lifted everyone's spirit and encouraged the French king to continue resisting, which resulted in the eventual ousting of the English from France.

But Joan was never destined to see the final victory. Captured by the French but loyal to the English, she was accused of heresy and burned at the stake. The French king did nothing to arrange for her release. In 1920, the Catholic Church officially recognized Joan of Arc as a saint.

What are you willing to sacrifice in response to your life's purpose? Is your passion deep enough to accomplish your task? Ready! Aim! Fire!

I make plans and carry them out. I have understanding, and I am strong.

Proverbs 8:14

CHAPTER 12

A FIGHT TO THE END

Born in 69 BC, Cleopatra was the last in the line
of Pharaohs to rule Egypt. Belonging to the Ptolemy
dynasty, she was supposed to rule Egypt alongside
her younger brother, Ptolemy XIII, but the sibling
rivalry would dictate otherwise. Rather than
submitting herself to her brother's will, as the
custom dictated, she decided to grab all the power in
a desperate attempt to restore Egypt to its former
glory. In a land beset by ruthless enemies and torn
apart by inner strife and natural disasters, Cleopatra
had to turn towards the most powerful ally she could
find – Gaius Julius Caesar.

[A Story within a Story]

"My queen, it's not going to work," said her
faithful servant, Apollodorus. "Ptolemy's palace is
heavily guarded and everyone coming and going is
thoroughly checked. We have no way to contact
Caesar, let alone arrange a meeting between the two
of you, at least not while he's staying at the palace."

Cleopatra rose from the seat and couldn't help but notice the desperate situation she was in. "How quickly the wheel of fortune turns!" she thought. "Just a few months ago, I was living in splendor, but now I'm clinging to the very last shreds of hope. I can't help but fight to the very end."

She approached the window and looked at the flickering lights that dotted the palace across the canal. "He's so near; I can't give up now," she whispered to herself. "My queen?" Apollodorus leaned in. Cleopatra turned around to face him. She felt her royal dignity come back and spoke in a calm voice that didn't tolerate disobedience, "We will take a boat and quietly cross the canal. And bring a carpet with us."

"A carpet, my queen?" said Apollodorus with a puzzled expression. "Yes, it will be a gift worthy of Caesar," she said with a faint smile on her face.

Ptolemy's guards inside the palace knew Apollodorus well. They considered him a suck-up that clings on to his former influence and glory and switches masters as the wind changes. Still, the guards had a profoundly ingrained sense of respect for anyone wielding any amount of authority.

"Apollodorus, you old rag, where are you lugging that old rug?" shouted a guard and made his partner burst out laughing. Apollodorus pretended he wasn't offended by this jab, but made a mental note to repay these guards someday. "This is a present for Caesar himself, and I shall give it to him in person," said Apollodorus, as beads of sweat glistened on his forehead.

"A present?" said the guard cheerily and smacked the carpet with his palm. "Sure, go right ahead." Apollodorus heard a faint cry of pain from inside the carpet as he rushed towards the guest room while trying to keep his pace steady.

Once inside Caesar's quarters, Apollodorus unfurled the carpet and Cleopatra emerged in all her beauty, like a bird spreading its wings after a storm. Caesar put down the reports he was reading and said with a smile, "Apollodorus, you may leave us now. Cleopatra and I have important matters to discuss."

Despite giving birth to Caesar's son, Cleopatra was unable to save Egypt. Caesar's desire to marry Cleopatra and proclaim himself a king came to an abrupt end after the Roman Senate heard about his decision. Therefore, a plan for his assassination was put into place and executed. Soon after, Cleopatra realized that she had no more allies remaining. Defiant as any other Pharaoh, she fought to the end.

Is there something that you will fight for to the end? Have you counted the cost? What is stopping you? The power you possess is stronger than the weakness you may feel. In life, you will face setbacks, obstacles, and feelings of defeat. But there is no reason to throw in the towel.

The race is not given to the swift nor the strong, but to those who endure to the end.
- Anonymous

VALERIE SHERROD

CHAPTER 13

THE POWER TO BE ME

There are many powerful inspirational words in the world today that are relevant in discussions pertaining to the power to be oneself, but there is one that really should matter. It is a quote from Oscar Wilde which says, "Be yourself; everyone else is already taken."

Sometimes you may feel intimidated or controlled by the opinions of others about you. Still, having made a decision to be hardworking, or to achieve your dreams by any means, there comes that fear that people may criticize you…that you may not perform according to others expectations. Perhaps, you really want to imitate someone else – a popular jockey or model who is entirely different from the person you are – and you are going to extreme measures to become that person. If this is the case, it is obvious; you don't realize that power resides in being true to who you are or who you can become, regardless of what others might think about you. Power also resides in the ability to face one's fears head on, starting from the belief that you embody the strength of a champion by believing in yourself or you can decide to be your own worst enemy.

Let's get straight to the point. According to Rita Mae Brown, "all you can do in life is to be who you are. Some people will love you for you, most will love you for what you can do for them, and some won't like you at all." Thus, it is important to live each day, knowing that whatever you do, be able to live with the choices you make. This is where the power resides because the moment you realize that you are who you are and not a replica of someone else, everything begins to make a whole lot of sense.

So back to the powerful quote from Oscar Wilde – be yourself! The truth is. you may try but you cannot be someone else. They may also try but they cannot be you. Power resides in the effort to be oneself, no matter the situation. You want to become a professional at something? Do it your way! You want to achieve a few goals before the year ends? Do it your way! You want to start a relationship with someone? Do it your way! It is unwise and emotionally unhealthy to alter who you are just to make people around you happy.

Moreover, it is human nature to consider others. It is what the word "empathy" means – learning to consider the feelings of others. I believe people

80   VALERIE SHERROD

should do what is in their power to assist others, but not at the expense of being manipulated. Be good to yourself first, create your own inner sanctuary, then allow others into your world exactly as you have built it and not as they expect it to be.

This inspirational piece would be incomplete without a quote from Maya Angelou which reads that "you may not control all the events that happen to you, but you can decide not to be reduced by them." So, stand up for yourself, be present and allow the power to be you manifest in your daily life.

There is great power to be oneself. There is great power to be you. That power, amongst many, is the zeal to live the life of your dreams without fear.

DARE TO BE
DIFFERENT

CHAPTER 14

MIRROR MIRROR ON THE WALL

How you perceive yourself, your hopes and dreams, and things you feel and think about reflect hugely on your self-image. Many people have asked themselves these questions: "What do I want in life?" "What have I done throughout my life?" "How do I look in other people's eyes?" These self-image questions can be positive or negative, inspiring confidence in your thoughts and actions, or making you doubtful of your ideas and capabilities.

Fortunately, the way you see yourself can be different from how others see you. There are people who, on the outside, appear to have everything working for them (big house, good looks, financial and personal success, and intelligence) but in reality, they may have a terrible self-image. Similarly, others have had multiple hardships in life, yet, have a very positive self-image.

Some believe that a person's self-image is determined by their environment or their position in life that influences him or her (*e.g.*, success in career, school, or relationships). There might be some truth to both beliefs. Undoubtedly, your self-image plays a vital role in your outlook on life and your happiness, which can rub off on those around you. If you aim for a positive self-image, people are more likely to see you as a confident and happy person.

Nonetheless, it's essential that your self-image is realistic and positive too. Having a self-image that is unrealistic can become a liability. When a person is so hung up on "going with the crowd," their self-image gets lost in the crowd, and they become someone else. Being realistic and not becoming someone else makes you a much happier person. As a result, you are no longer living in self-denial or 'the prison of the individual you are not!' Being self-critical occasionally is not too bad; it can lead to perseverance, hard work, change, growth, and success. Find the balance between feeling positive about yourself and setting realistic goals.

Women sometimes feel the need to hide behind a mask. Doing so might end up hurting you more than you think. A mask is a standard covering for women. We love makeup, beautiful clothes, and all the trimmings. These things are camouflage. Until you face challenging situations, where your self-image is tested, then you will discover you don't need your mask to be self-confident. As you develop, you will see that you don't need anyone's validation or anything else to feel positive about yourself.

Your positive self-image creates the space for you to be who you say you are. Never let anyone tell you contrary, and never let anyone stop you from being who you are. Be yourself!

"When she speaks, her words are wise, and she gives instructions with kindness."

Proverbs 31:26

CHAPTER 15

NO GREATER LOVE

God has always chosen to describe his relationship with humanity regarding a courtship, culminating in a wedding, without omitting the ardor and passion of such a relationship. This we see most clearly in the Song of Solomon, a little-read and even less understood book with content that makes some people blush. In very graphic, erotic language, two lovers share a deep passion for one another. The passion we witness between two lovers is symbolic of how God describes his love for people and the kind of passionate response he expects from them in return.

Yes, God loves us. But, have we ever stopped to consider the depth and the fervor of His love for us? Reading this book should be an eye-opener, as he describes his longing for the embrace of his beloved. Then we get a vivid picture of how passionately we are loved and metaphorically intimate with the Divine.

He declares us as his beloved, his dove, and the one who has ravished his heart thoroughly and whose love he considers as better than wine. Wow! This is God telling you how much he loves you and wants to be in a relationship with you. As a woman, who can resist such romance!

In return, God wants us to be equally passionate about him and respond ardently to his romantic overtures. He does not hesitate to comment on the beauty of us, including our beloved, feet, thighs, navel, nose, and breasts. This is intimate and personal, and the metaphoric meaning is deep, expressing his love for us, just like an excited bridegroom on his honeymoon. He sees us as pure through His Son, Jesus Christ.

The question is—how do you feel about all this? God wants you to know that you are special, no matter how you look physically or what weaknesses you may have. You are loved with a love that is stronger than human love and with a thirst that water cannot quench. Remember this every time you look in the mirror or feel less than adequate, and ask him to give you just as passionate love for him as he has for you. He, your first love, desires to do this.

I am my beloved and His desire is toward me
Song 7:10 (NKJV)

VALERIE SHERROD

MY BELOVED DAUGHTERS

*How do I express my love for that which is Divine
Spark of Me? How do I describe the ways in which I
cherish your beautiful souls, so radiant with light and
love, and yet so fragile and vulnerable
are your sweet, sweethearts?
How do I let you know that despite the
challenges and sorrows that you face,
that I am always by your side
filling you with My Grace and My Sacred Divinity?*

*So brave you were to take on the human condition;
to step up to another incarnation filled with such
varied experiences that I may share with you!
How I love, honor and respect all that you have
sacrificed in My name.*

*My daughters, you are My prayer,
the forerunners of the chaos that signifies life;
my best and most devoted disciples!
Please allow Me to gift you daily with the stillness of
being so that you may connect with Spirit
and be reminded that all is well
despite your frustrations and challenges;
Despite the abundant energy of the Earthbound.
Allow me to water you, as I would all of my beautiful
flowers, with the stillness of Soul and the jewels of
non-attachment, for it is in non-attachment
that you will find peace.*

*I pray you understand that I am always guiding you
to the wisdom that allows you to see how deserving
you are of this Fathers love.
At all times, I pour forth respect and honor into the
beautiful vessels that house the Divine Spark of Me.*

VALERIE SHERROD

I wish to celebrate with you this experience called life
that you have chosen to endure
and I bless your unselfish desire to become an active
participant in this incredible journey.

Know that I hold you Sacred in the palm of My
hands, in the deepest, safest place of My Being,
and that forever and always
you have My devotion and My love.

As every father knows, and I am no different,
we are not capable of keeping you
from experiencing the panorama of life.
What you experience you have asked for,
before coming into human form
and I wish for you to know that
I sanctify your courage, your devotion to life and
your never-ending, all-encompassing desires
to make the world a better place.

YOUR DEVOTED SPIRITUAL FATHER

TITLES BY VALERIE SHERROD

Books

By Any Deceptive Means Necessary/Obstacles that
    Prevent Women from Fulfilling their Destiny
Pussy Power
The 90 Day Author
The No-Nonsense Guide to Self-Publishing

Magazines
Couleure Fashion Magazine

Comic Books
Dominion12 – Super Hero Kids Against Bullying
Global Warming – Think Like a Kid
Patience and the Pirates

REFERENCES

Lang, Ilene H. (2014), *"Companies With More Women Board Directors Experience Higher Financial Performance, According to Latest Catalyst Bottom Line Report,"* accessed 1 May 2017, <https://www.catalyst.org/media/companies-more-women-board-directors-experience-higher-financial-performance-according-latest>.

The Power to Be Me p. 79 (Quotes were drawn from): Seale, Quincy (2018), *"Quotes About Being Yourself,"* accessed 1 January 2019, <https://www.keepinspiring.me//quotes-about-being-yourself>.

ABOUT THE AUTHOR

Valerie Sherrod is an entrepreneur, author, book publishing strategist, graphic designer, and humanitarian.

She is also considered a multi-gifted artist who is also known for her wisdom and sense of humor.

The author is also the founder of Femini Publishing and Enterprises, which focuses on the different aspects of her publishing empire, including The 90 Day Author, The 90 Day Author Kids and Couleure Fashion Magazine.

Valerie has worked with many authors to get their works in print by navigating the challenging, yet rewarding process.

Passionate about what she does, Valerie has taught life skills to women and teenagers, engaged in foreign missions, and has aided in the development of leaders and entrepreneurs by implementing strategies for success.

I AM DIVINE

"I praise you because I am fearfully and wonderfully made."

Psalm 139:14

www.ingramcontent.com/pod-product-compliance
Lightning Source LLC
LaVergne TN
LVHW051701080426
835511LV00017B/2662